THE BEAUTIFUL
CONTRADICTIONS

NEW DIRECTIONS POETRY PAMPHLETS

Nathaniel Tarn

THE BEAUTIFUL
CONTRADICTIONS

New Directions Poetry Pamphlet #5

The Beautiful Contradictions was first published in 1969 by Cape Goliard Press Ltd., London, UK, and in 1970 by Random House, New York.

Cover design by Office of Paul Sahre
Interior design by Erik Rieselbach
Manufactured in the United States of America
New Directions Books are printed on acid-free paper
First published as New Directions Poetry Pamphlet #5 in 2013
Published simultaneously in Canada by Penguin Books Canada Limited

Library of Congress Cataloging-in-Publication Data
Tarn, Nathaniel.
[Poems. Selections]
The beautiful contradictions / Nathaniel Tarn.
pages ; cm. — (New Directions poetry pamphlet ; #5)
ISBN 978-0-8112-2095-8 (acid-free paper)
I. Title.
PS3570.A635B4 2013
811'.54—dc23

2013005434

10 9 8 7 6 5 4 3 2 1

New Directions Books are published for James Laughlin
by New Directions Publishing Corporation
80 Eighth Avenue, New York, NY 10011

"I will start afresh and bring everything into light ..."
                                        —*Oedipus Rex*

"Es la hora de los hornos y no se ha de ver más que la luz."
                                        —José Martí

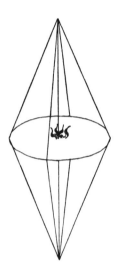

ONE

To cease working in shadow with the light against us
no longer concerned with the fate of any particular element
thrashing to emerge from swaddling cloths
since the problem is to love all without loss of edge
from particular   the uses of   to general   the uses of
to work in the naked light with elation   extreme elation

and once the experiment has begun to make an end of it
so that no frontiers whatsoever be accredited
with heart and mind agreed on the minimal solutions
necessary for each individual to live under a roof
with clean air   clean food   clean water   clean time to use
working in open light   elated   hard   sharp   put it diamond-like   for

it is a myth you know that desire dissolves all obstacles
it has never been known to dissolve mountains at all
and should the most violent fire you can imagine melt one
nevertheless another would grow up precisely in the same place
and the landscape look exactly the same as it did before
because there is no end to the production and destruction of mountains

This is the discipline required of us now
whether we have   or not   any chance of success
we have no alternative to taking the whole world as our mother
since no one can pretend to own anything of permanence
or to anchor her roots in any particular plot
or speak in anything but borrowed languages

Every time we arrive at a new place
we grope about in it as roots must grope in the earth
look for the detail will seem to make us its owner
but by the time the leaves turn away from the sun
we have almost forgotten the tongue we spoke to break silence
our origin holes are covered with stones

Tell us this mountain is no longer the tallest of mountains
the tree-lines have moved up or down so many hundred feet
say these grass plains have become a desert
this trail has not been walked in living memory
the last of these animals laid itself down before our birth
these are no longer our boundaries

Nevertheless we recite the old world because we own it in our souls
and when we tell its places in their proper order
we are sickened to death by the illusions we have about mine and thine
the skin we wear having been designed to fit each one of us
and never for a moment tailored to mask any particular race
the covenant hacked out of it once and for all   the flesh saved

It is up to me   since I must lose myself   to call them one by one
wearing these tattered fragments of the human skin
to persuade them that from time to time they must think of filial duties
such as bringing the relics together at the cremation pyre
drawing a human shape on a piece of ground
lying still in the waters surrounded with light

I shall have to pass through every birth   every occasion of birth

                              so that the river turn of its own accord

the waters run back to break

                              out from her all at once

it is up to me to call into being everything there is

TWO

His vomit in my mouth
my neck wet with his snot
his breath over my face
his blood coughed on my knees
his shit on my toes
and I have spared you the details fellow-students
of blood-brother relations
I   rain-priest of Atitlán   Ralkoal Zutuhil
and that   not just for one night   many years ago   as a travel memento

but for years your poverty on my hands   alcaldes   juezes   regidores
alguaciles   telineles   tisheles   señores y señoras mios y mias
great lords   great ladies still in your stink of sick and pine
for years waking at dawn with wooden buttocks on a narrow bench
insomnia's ache lining my face   a needle in every vein
to drink the nose-twisting traguito
or smoke to the greater glory of the lord Simon Judas Iscariot

who is also San Pedro of the keys and cocks   alias Pedro de Alvarado
conquistador of Tziquinahá   in Quauhtemallan   for Spain
alias San Miguel Arcángel   lord of the winds and hills
alias Mam the ancient of days   the year's thrombosis
male and female when young   plural   screwing themselves in caves
then fainting downwind to the sea   with plaintive cries
to macerate into old Mam once more   to crucify the year

I danced like a bear to the greater glory of the puppet
which never flared at Easter but was worshipped more than Jesucristo
taken back and dismembered into his bundle after the Friday procession
where all the winds in the world come out if the door is left open
where we lie down in the arms of the many-colored maize
praying that Mam should move   that the world be not left in silence
since fathers now walk out of step with their sons

When the padres had come to steal the bundles and masks
relegated the great doll to the pig-pound for three years
he who walked the world like a dream to give men lovers
while the elders went mad at their village dying
we took the case of the elders against the young politicos
as far as the president of the republic and won our case
because you do not take the heart out of men without some reparation

Great lords it is time you knew it
Huracán   the heart of heaven   thinks again
summons his siblings from their beds of green and blue feathers
where they lie in the water surrounded with light
saying that all the creations have been eliminated time and again
because they failed to break silence and praise the heart of heaven
the animals who hissed   screamed   cackled   but could not speak names
the men of clay who drooped back into clay
the men of wood who walked on all fours but had no minds
destroyed by the cardinal weathers   earth   water   air   and fire

                              but he is saying now that he will destroy by oblivion

dear gods as if I had never spoken

          Maltiosh te-e-taa   maltiosh alcalde   maltiosh primero   'tiosh 'tiosh

the heart of seas   the heart of lakes   the heart of sky   are still
the green plate is flawed   the blue gourd broken
foxes   pigs   hunting bitches   bleed from their noses

                                             the Lord has given

the book of the mother-fathers cannot be seen any more
the skull-tree drips no more semen for our mothers' vaginas
no one has gone down into the bowels of fire   to bring back sons

'tiosh 'calde   'tiosh primero   'tiosh secundo 'tiosh

contract your bellies old men   let the world breathe by
pull in your navels all over again for the stones to boil in the dark
goodbye to the gods until that long meal is over   that pie of generations

                                             the Lord has taken away

blessed be the name of the Lord   who thinks again

But my having everything   you having nothing at all
the pain that causes me puts me in the way very nicely
of doing my job effectively while paying the minimum in taxes

thank you father   why should it ever end father   when exactly father
this being after all such a *rich* exile
I like it so much down here

and for every corner of the earth where someone is in pain or dying
there is another corner where you will find the same
no grain of sand as small as the last pain to be tracked down

                        I make a meal of it all   I spew it out again

dear gods as if you had never spoken

THREE

We shall make a very long poem of it all of us together
and to this end you must now agree that you shall be my mothers
expanding the category in all directions to include from time to time
certain brothers and husbands of mothers or other such males
since we can never achieve the undiluted rule of women
and further I shall assume a filial stance toward you
leaving no one able to hold that I am not a prince   a gentleman
or that any right I could claim to the throne might be invalid

Harshness might come of it in our line   though it softens the fathers
and the yielding of all of you to my will might make amends
when I come of age to lord it at last as a pillar of granaries
I shall make you stand in for the whole world and its creatures
buried in you   one after another   I shall lie in all beings
having no land otherwise on which to lay my head
no pillow from which to see the trees bowing like elephants along the wall
as they did in my childhood nights   when I bled white

only pretending once in a while that you are all one woman
as my hands reach for your hands to dispose them on you   on I
in every exchange that we can calculate   as far as hands can wed
before I grow into you without effort   as a tree grows through rock
with the length of time it takes to do away with force
before you grow into me   as water flows over rock
with the length of time it takes to do away with force
only pretending once in a while that you are all one woman

Afloat in the warm straights between your legs   the Hercules pillars
my day and your night have married the world
linking our continents in one surge toward the ocean
the articulation of the waves teaches us motion
the cripple in the waves persevering in his efforts to flow
gradually getting the curve of it and toppling over himself
breaking his neck like a racehorse on the still shores
tucking his own assent under himself to be crippled again

We worship the noise of the sea   its everlasting language
its efforts as unceasing as war
since there is only one creature in all our realms
which can go on naming itself over and over
without fatigue of any kind   discourtesy   or sense of imposition
or wanting to lie down after work   or stop to rest
I took you once as my slave in the long waves
as we spread out of the inland sea over the cold Atlantic

once the waves had started that way they were never to be still again
until Europe had spawned across the American continent
killing everything in sight there in the names of lebensraum and liberty
shipping you my mothers to replace the local stock
Now prairie wheat leans in the wind over Pacific waters
the far west of America raises harvests on Asia
bone harvests in the name of liberty only
and carrion feeds the Californian mills

The smell of that wheat came over Pequod as she was hunting
but nothing shamed or troubled her course else
now the locusts have come out of the ground with their eyes like moons
to eat men
the locusts piss fire in fine sprays over forest and jungle
the locusts spit fire bouncing along the ground
their antennae plague every skin they touch
the sky is never free from their noise

and for every child that dies   irrespective of the cause
for everyone without anything left to look out from behind its eyes
after sucking the blood from its mother's pap
millions are dying on the prairies without their own knowledge
the streets from New York to San Francisco are littered with dead
we mourn the America of Whitman and Melville
we are ashamed for America
we mourn our prodigal   our Absalom   we must conceive new races

Nor is it over yet
because for all you know the khans heave again under their hills
and the waves must continue to roll until they bring to us
where a new Greece   a new Egypt   a new Israel   are sprouting
the very freshness I eye you with my mothers to whom I am making love
while the wild seeds tumble again together in your bellies
the animals come in from the dark to the byres in our sheets
our bodies of brine turn to bodies of bread

You will stand before the hordes tumbling this way
our royal self hardly born still attached to you by the belly
you will give us birth in the dust raised by their hooves
stain the earth with the four colors of man and of maize
the tribes shall come together for fresh parleys at dawn
dictate their new interpretations of our common earth
I shall remember the waters where I lay   surrounded with light
our long voyage together   rocking the sea

FOUR

My job she told us   with some solemnity
is to lift the myth like a bandage from his eyes
to show him that only in imagination have I ever been his mother
(mother-marriage won't work in theory and is bound to be rough in practice
we don't marry our mothers   sisters   daughters   cousins   because
we exchange them for other men's women)
so look I said she told us   stop looking at me this way if you can
to show him that only in imagination had I ever been his mother
but made small progress

He had never set eyes on a woman before   had gone on hearsay
to guess those breasts a trifle ripe now signaled me the creature
marching up that mountain spiral martially as he did
and me so cold lying there for the vultures to defile
that circle of fire about me as useless as an English heater
his eyes were closed   I'd say he was dreaming just as I was dreaming
who had prophecied his birth in his real mother's womb
before my father kissed the splendor off my eyes
so how *could* we be the same woman for heaven's sake   and yet

I wonder whether we're ever going to have some breakfast in the Ring
eggs and bacon at sunrise   for instance   or have to leave the room
(both possibilities to ease an audience into sympathy)
Why not a production on those lines without the long discussions
the singers going through a day at home from rise to lie me down
with breakfasts and sitting in real toilets when need be
all that very much of course while they sing
because it is a myth you know that desire dissolves all obstacles
while feeding and singing keep our figures redundant

i.   He kills his father on the way up the mountain
ii.   he sees a woman killed by his father
iii.   seeing a woman for the first time he is surprised and thinks her mother
iv.   she has to dissuade him but he is not really fooled
v.   they agree that the unreality of art is unreliable
vi.   he blinds himself in the traditional manner
vii. her breasts soak his feet in milk
viii. he treads his milk into hers
ix.   at the top of the stairs all her mouths open to sing

I say he blinded himself because he was beginning to guess I'm not the one
as I stood at the top of the stairs he received me entirely
received me like a host and devoured me
from the top of the stairs I looked down at him and laughed
with the whole of his god in his mouth
all my doors were opening to give out food and drink
I was feeding the needy and comforting the sick
far beyond the circle of the burning mountain
the fields began to warm again under a blanket of harvests

Perhaps he knew that he had to go blind in order to speak
with any pretence at prophecy
to tell his own youth of the marriage it had contracted
on that dusty crossroads where the gods were waiting
he goes down now into everything that his mother once made
out there among the fields where plants grow by her virtue
no one will ever mine the coal in her eyes
the diamonds glisten on her singing throat
she gives its birth to everything there is

                      by our father's will I am made his bride

FIVE

Looking into the eyes of babies in experiments
born without the normal pressure on their skulls
thinking they are going to put an end to philosophy
when some development of this begins to breed monsters
and that the chase through probability of the genius
the great kick he gives through his mother as he comes out
the clarity of the air surrounding him later in life
however much his body might take revenge on him
his mind crack between the diameter of his skull and the crown

                    reality comprises

that the immeasurable heave of the whole race
to bring this animal to the tree's crest and enthrone it there
may be gone forever in a moment of medical history
like the passing of some art   or an old migration
of all the birds together in the arms of the same wind
the way the planet used to turn in one direction with one purpose

                    frightens a lot

I remember on the shores of the most beautiful lake in the world
whose name in its own language means abundance of waters
as if the volcanoes surrounding it had broken open the earth
there in the village of Saint James of Compostela one cold night
not the cereus-scented summer nights in which a voice I never traced
sang those heartbreaking serenades to no one known
a visiting couple gave birth in the market place
the father gnawing the cord like a rat to free the child
and before leaving in the morning they were given the freedom of the place

                    I mean the child was given

SIX

Not one world this   but fractions of all possible worlds this
again   not science this   nor the mind in movement on its elected paths
exhibiting work sprung from a center fashioned by you alone
Mr. Rex I have been quarrying in the night and it has taken all my strength
to come up again from those depths with anything I can use
you know as well as I do how hazy it all seems in the morning
you can't solder together those connections so clear in sleep
it is very hard to detain the present Mr. Rex   maybe harder with eyes
as I learned once when I searched among the lower orders for a wife
and looking death in the eyes lost my wife forever

I had seen her whole that once when we were introduced
as I never saw her whole again
by the time she had committed the indiscretion she was dragged down for
she was little more to me than a collection of odd limbs
when I went down to get her back it was really a question of decency
more than anything you could call love since love makes whole
The second chance I was given meant having her whole in the mind alone
on condition I should never look back to check against the facts
life being unbearable   of course   at some elbow in the rock
I did turn round for the whole prize and that was that

Have you ever been able to make anything of this notion of piecemeal murder
I have never set eyes on this person in my life
as you stumbled on the greasy roads   a daughter on each arm
our cars passed through the center of town to avoid the station
reflecting on the magnificent noises you could make with your eyes out
a few times   yes   to attend the sick
thinking forward to whatever else the gods could do to man
separating those fit for work from those unfit
say one takes a hand and puts a nail through that (instead of eyes)
it was never the task of the medical staff to herd them in

another feet and puts a nail through them   a third one testicles
such concerns were purely administrative   a matter of orders
nail after nail through each live part of the inhabited earth
on one occasion   the orderly being sick   I turned on the taps
well each one says of his nail that it is only hurting a little bit
I was supposed to choose the subjects for my superiors to inject
and that his own nail could not conceivably do any harm by itself
on a single occasion I injected a woman myself   yes   saw her fall
while group responsibility is something that went out with the Jews

Between mishap and mishap Mr. Rex you know how easy it is to die

SEVEN

Dawn wind   the birds sing out   born of the wind
light wakes the hills as they fall in upon us
the trees collapse into the valley's arms
my side is open   now be my rib
now open yours   and let me make your cage

my only house   Here I have touched the earth
followed familiar animals
fed faithful visitors among the birds
Ah   all these creatures need their watering
and I   their father   have been a parching sun

But here   at Singing-Birds   light floods my brain
as mist fills out the ribbing in the valley's sides
it is no matter now of knowing how some joy
would have been joy indeed   had I been capable
had I not been of desert   and of sand compounded

but   this is joy   joy now   immediately
What then shall be the fate of these particular
attachments to one place   to one impediment
I answer how the mist one day   combining with the sun
gloried a single larch   left all the others dark

the wind-whipped tussocks bounced like spinning tops
the mosses gleamed like emeralds in their mines
the lichen curled its feathers round the stones
and   in the air   the buzzard cried on me
crowning the valley in his spiral flight

In such a fire   men once saw angels walk

EIGHT

It happened once   in an unwilling but fascinated way
some aberration of the collector's instinct having overtaken me
that I was responsible for the destruction of a fragment of history
a fingernail dislodging a minute particle from a fresco
some one thousand five hundred years old at the very least
the particle   as I should have expected   falling away in powder
There were six monks who had come down from the mountains at the time
as monks had probably been coming for one thousand five hundred years
they waited for the tourists to leave each cave
and then went in to bow to everyone of the Buddhas
with great piousness and no concern at all for their aesthetic value

There were a great many Buddhas there   small and large
though not as many as there are persons or blades of grass not to be saved
sand-grains   water-traces   light-particles   not to be saved
and taken into an inexistent Nirvāna by an inexistent Bodhisattva
that is if you understand the great armor of the Prajñāpāramitā
Then the six monks returning walked round the tourist buses
took the proceeds   bought with wide smiles a plateful of fish
which they ate with wide smiles as they might have eaten a seventh monk
I do not believe that I have ever been so moved in my life by any men
or felt that I was so close to the origins of compassion
or to the skin of patience I had scratched by misrule

The destruction of history by not setting down the history one knows
by refusing to be a witness to one's times is a crime against the earth
in this I have done some wrong by failing the history of the Sangha
refusing to write the history of one section for busyness
though that section *were* located in a relatively insignificant culture
a suburb of Asia   very ugly into the bargain   not to mention pretentious
no limb of the great East I dreamed   my childhood bride
yet inalienably part of the field of merit in which we sow our deeds
Somewhere in the billowing robe between Sarnath and Kyōto
among the incalculable elements of stuff in that time-quenching garment
the smallest gash bears witness   the smallest rent unrepaired

It is made worse by the knowledge that much of the Sangha is dead or dying
the Sangha of the four quarters flourishes only among museums
the mystic East you love is as good as pickled
new people are being heaped on new people   and being chosen
most urgently by history without concern for lineage
from Vladivostok to Xinjiang the settlers are squatting
all along the twenty-six thousand mile border   give or take a mile
the provinces   the counties   the heavenly shires the Russians took
as imperialist in their time as the worst of the breed
are being contested   maps out   banners up   the tribes drinking tea
now with one side   now with the other

The musics are being composed   the slogans set to music
to teach us hate for what we had come to love
painfully slowly because it is at the other end of the earth
and love is very hard to bear when it has so far to go
as you know when you weep for Aberfan   a little less for Vietnam
What good have the Waleys   Pounds   Perses   and Segalens been
Chavannes   Granets   Steins   and Groussets been
who have given their lives to the study of the middle earth
or Fenellosa   whom some of you admire as a critic
if there be some   writers at that   I know
to drink willingly until two a.m. arguing the East never matched

Saint Thomas Aquinas or Dante or other equally respectable persons
there being in such a case nothing like a relevant East
not to mention all the Chinese   Japanese   Indians   *et al*
who have tried to tell their people about Aquinas   Dante   you
if it is all to begin again at the drop of a treaty on a larger scale
and for that matter why did I have to remain in exile
years in the West   years in the East
if we are to be taught again laboriously the habits of hate
if all that mingles in the end will be our plasma
There is no worthier subject for poetry in our time
than the fear that the races should rise and rend each other

our mother the earth should forget herself   her milk run dry

NINE

Sweeping up the leaves today we whip up a sea stir about our feet
the swish of leaves going this way then that   this way then that
ever more leaves out of the gullies   the lips of lawns
off the paths and terraces toward the garden's navel
until it looks as if blood is swirling around our feet
The leaves are coming down from other trees than ours
we understand that garden borders are by no means national frontiers
leaves are coming in from the outermost suburbs all over the city
even from the countryside we suspect to thicken this pile
blood runs out of every vein   the earth's pelt dries under foot
there should be privileged work like this to do for poets
since it is only in working that ideas come at all

When you swim in the sea of leaves it seems huge
you have the feeling you must be in communion with all of nature
imagining the Yangtse   the Mississippi   the Amazon   in full flood
or the turbulence of the great deeps   the trenches   the whale hangars
as far as under the icecap where the beasts brood
winter away after this flood of leaves
and whence they are ejected into summer seas
nuzzled by huge placentas full of anemones and fish
That is assuming you are unaware of what silence condones
because the cry of Sodom and Gomorrah is great   their sin very grievous
there go the blubber ships   plagues of leviathan
Norwegians amortized   Russians half-through   the Japanese determined

their ships so nearly new   their profits untilled
In the name of the Buddha then or Amitābha of the western paradise
whose compassion is almost the sum of good in your culture
in the names of your own dead in two holocausts
so that our children need not be disinherited in a world of humans only
do not bring down the pillars of this world
Wilt thou destroy the righteous with the wicked   not one just whale
even humanely   leaving the whale to sport in the poet's mind alone
When you swim in the sea of leaves it appears huge   what   not one whale
but when you stand away from the sea you have caused to flow about us
and survey the accumulation from a safe distance on the beach
the pile of leaves looks small for all the work that has gone into it

TEN

How poor yet how beautiful you are
Madonna in your snows condemned to childlessness
blindfold   broken-staffed   with a young girl's figure
never fated to sail   to billow like the moon
how poor   how dignified you are
though I must meet you at these alien gates
in a stone dialect I never spoke since we are not carvers
nor makers of images to imitate the coming and going of God
how poor   how solitary you stand
not as one of a pair   yet defined by that relation
though every tourist buys his picture of you   not of the other
and one suspects more and more that a Jew broke the rule
to make you synagogue of Strasbourg   beside the smirking church

Turned toward Germany on this soil which is neither Germany nor France
modestly waiting for your sons to be   that cannot be now
much less indeed than they could ever be
since testicles and ovaries were destroyed in Germany
not many years ago   and by some that visit you now
turned toward eastern Europe where my own blood was poured
into Freud   Einstein   Marx   outlasting fire
to shape this time we are bent on discussing now
how you seem to yearn for me sometimes as if I were a lover
and how I yearn for you in my bowels   mother of Zion   bride of need
Let us talk a little of days gone by in the wooden towns
where the poor were scholars   every son a prince
mothers bent over cradles calling their babies saints

never was black joy's color so much as in those towns
alphabet black   scholars' robes   crows
sitting upon black trees   their shawls of sky about them
never poverty such a virtue as it was in those courts
where cartwheel hats poured over the laws
and the holy danced like blades whenever letters moved
never singing so guileless as when a cantor sang
alone as if the Lord were stroking his tail
while tier on tier of cloud fell to expose the heavens

never matter so rent to show the spirit through
as when the leaves on every tree conspired to whisper praise
and no one could tell tree from book   or book from tree
past and future being so welded together   time of such paltry account

This is new language   this is new language   listen
life is admirable life is admirable   it is vain said the rabbi of Strasbourg
it is the heart   it is the light   it is the leaves   it is the law
nothing preceding   nothing conceding   nothing future   nothing now
but instant laid beside instant like shoes along a wall
Lord I have seen time lie down with time said he
in the thighs of Zion I have myself lain down
Lord I have seen the beginnings conversing with the conclusions
in our very language   the book's black tongues
Lord you were old again   white-bearded   gowned in sky
my bride and I brushed by you in the midst of the garden
our hair made of gold   the fountain   the apple
indeed everything that was not blue   green   or flesh

or red of the four-winged fire that showed us out of the garden
in the very same picture   the rich hours   the lord of Berry's
another goy   dear God   but you disallowed us ourselves
so that we have become as the little fish that live in deep caves
I know because it all began in Strasbourg said the rabbi of Strasbourg
who had been made rabbi by this alien hand when he saw the blind girl
and from then on rocked in any temple left standing in Europe
to begin with in the Staronová   the bear-pit of Prague
where he was nabbed for coppers like a Jew
honored to clutch the law   joined on a Saturday
in crying raus to a party of Germans who had insisted on straying in
glorying in the right to cry raus to the Germans
in what was after all no more than the museum we have become

Adolf Hitler had settled on a museum in Praha
the Gestapo sent tatters and silver from all Israel
at the liberation there was no time to destroy them
I survive in my rags in Praha the slender
I rock like a dinosaur on the sweating stones

Franz who had seen the golem in these streets rocks with me
and the great rabbi Low who had made the golem
we talk of our fathers on the flagstones of the Staronová
the oldest shrine of this administration in Europe now
since the destruction of medieval Wurms
Madonna of Strasbourg your ovaries are centuries old
your blood is dragon blood no longer bred in Europe
the blood of dragons has been shed at last

you have no more sons than the tribes have sons
and who will sing your songs in Babylon now
for there is no end to the production and destruction of mountains
Mahler could do it at one time   he is no longer with us   .
who will sing the Lord's song in a strange land   all land is strange
crouching here in the thirty-third year waiting for meteors
the same span of time as the Christ took to acquire his wisdom
somewhere in the eastern desert between Jerusalem and the Deccan
coming back all that way to put an end to the Jews
by being the last Jew   or so he thought   born of a Jewish mother
we matrilineal nanny-goats   an embarrassment to the Gentiles
poor in every art and wile like a one-legged radish
who managed nevertheless to exhaust the word

Well I can tell you that they are not messing around with my Kabbalah there
but keeping it under lock and key where it properly belongs
if there be no one qualified any longer to juggle the letters
the old cemetery has lost none of its teeth
German girls   who have wishes   as all girls do
drop disposable notice of their wishes in rabbi Loew's tomb
as indeed I have no doubt their fathers might have done
they swarm like flies   they buzz through the mist of the law
drawn by this ancient meat   this reptile broth
How poor yet how beautiful you are Madonna of Strasbourg
I summon the aleph sperm into my loins from the spine of God
I lie down in your stone hands my unforgotten
you shall have sons I swear it   on your blindness   on your eyes

The worm has made his way through books   how they crumble
fire his through the parchment of scholars' hides
the houses of study   their benches   tables   lights
are no longer as much as smoke in the sky   or a crow's feather
they have rubbed out our names from the library of the holy word
there is no longer method for me to ask your hand in marriage
no cloth to shield us from a rain of spears
when we wed in the blue light from everlasting to everlasting
I who face all ways   rocking here at the heart
will have purchased in the word a partnership with the Lord of hosts
made the races afresh before dawn on the sabbath's breath
I shall have time to spare beside you   I shall have time to spare
you shall have sons my love   unnumbered as the ghosts

ELEVEN

When Caesar decided to measure the world   as told in Hereford

a Cesare Augusto orbis terrarum metiri cepit   belted by Mors
Nicodoxus east   Polyclitus south   Theodotus north and west

there went out a decree from Caesar that the universe should be taxed
veici beu fiz mon piz dedeinz la quele chare preistes
e les mameleites dont leit de virgin queistes

while they from occidental pars   unknown among these maps
entered the womb of the old globe   along the hot equator
past Gades Herculis into the middle sea   there to survey
where they could find twelve labors   for to recruit the world

In the steps of the ancient stars   swilling the mermaid's milk
took Baleares first   Etna and Sandaliotes
harrowed the hells from Lipari   the cheapest way to do it
hugged bulls to death in Crete   decapitated Rhodes
stormed the white-windmilled Delos   sacked Chypre for wine

then sailed the Nile south-east   past Joseph's granaries
seized for themselves his seven years   stored in the pyramids
spun salamander's wool   plucked out Mandragora
suckled the Sphinx full-dry   smothered the spinster phoenix
tempted Saint Anthony under the burning mountain
sank out of human ken   to reach the outer Nile

enrolled the Agriophagi   their panther snacks   their king
the cheetah-swift Monocoli   the pouting tribes
the mouthless people who suck their food through reeds
Himantopodes creeping on all fours   the dwarfish Psyllii
the Blemmyae with sunken eyes and mouths   the Troglodytes
guzzling in caves and ignorant of speech   the ethnocentric ones
the Garamantes' mare who fetched the gold of ants

rose out of Carthage to harry Rome once more
shattered each scallop shell in golden Compostela
silenced the university of Paris   stopped Flanders looms
sank Britain in its own miasmata   anchored the Hebrides
(took rest at Carnau   place of singing birds
where I was staying   out of Hereford)
denied the Germans thrice   published the news in Prague
skewered a choir of Issedones   shared out their parents' limbs

tarried among the Hyperborei   who knew no sickness
taught these to look about them   at other peoples' problems
before they took the high jump to join the seven sleepers
gave emerald-guarding griffin some recent news of Wales
and smote on his behalf the one-eyed Arimaspi
enlisted the Albani   grey-pupilled   for the watch
and the bat-like Phanesii who sleep wrapped in their ears
crested por fin king Alexander's walls   in which he had imprisoned
the yellow Gog and Magog   the nightmares of his world

sat cuckoo-like among the pelicans drinking their father's blood
lulled by the sybil voice of a crimson Manticore
lived on the scent of apples among the bronzed Gangines
tried Amazons for paramours and found them wanting
lay in the shade of Sciapodes   under umbrella feet
inspected one small infantry warred on by cranes
tickled the crocodile between Chenab and Jhalum
propped up an elephant   his turret like a city
who swam them to Ceylon to prove his gratitude
covered by Avalerion   the fabled eagle pair

at last they circle Palestine   the navel of the world
landing on Sinai from the two-fingered sea
kiss Abraham's cheek as he leans out of Ur
weep with the wife of Lot   melt down her salt
walk the chameleon up Babylon's towers
flit with the Cinnamologus among cinnamon trees
ducking the fire-shit of angry Bonnacon
take tea at Ararat with lord and lady Noah
accept a flower wand from web-foot Tigolopes

the lynx's carbuncle against the royal pox
and bask at Troy   in fallen Helen's sheets

Now from corona mundi   Caesar in judgment sits
and in the hunter's mirror loses his cubs again
down from the buried rivers   under paradise
and from Saint Michael's eyes as he shuts down the east
a rain of spears fixes the stigmata
into the Carcass on hillock Calvarie
The dry tree withers   the dry tree waxes green
as the western lords survey Jerusalem
the twelve winds blow from the encompassed earth
the twelve apostles sing in the abundance of waters
as they lie in the Jordan surrounded with light
Jerusalem   the heart of heaven   shimmers among the waves

their losses have been few as yet   they are greenly remembered
Javier Heraud   poet   shot in Maldonado   Peru
Arbelio Ramirez   historian   in Montevideo
Camillo Torres   priest   in Chucuri   Colombia
Danilo Rosalez Arguello   doctor   in Matagalpa sierra
Jorge Vasquez Viana   poet   in the Bolivian sierra
Camillo Cienfuegos   doctor   drowned at sea   Cuba
Ramón Soto Castillo   professor   drowned in sky   Venezuela
Otto René Castillo   poet   burned alive   Guatemala
Ernesto Guevara   "prince"   deposed near Higueras
and other names that poetry cannot fit into last lines
they died as Jerusalem lay in the waters about us
ready to bud this year   their resurrected mother

TWELVE

When Coronado   according to Castañeda's observations   took New Granada
he was amazed by the Pueblo Indian conglomerations
the manifest identity of politics and ethics in these towns
that in some ways remind us now of the Greek city states
being impressed particularly with the uniformity of dwelling blocks
which seemed to present one several-storied wall to the exterior
accessible at the upper levels by means of ladders one could draw up
the impression of architectural unity reinforcing the concept of citizenship
by bodying forth the ideal Pueblo Indian as a man at one with his state
Now   if we think of it   the great city units of the past
are depicted in much the same visual language even in our dreams

the Babylons and Egypts of our visions are towered and storied
with infinite recessions as in John Martin's engravings
and even today we can be awed by medieval castle keeps
or by the white abyss of Lhasa's Potala
the cities we are in love with however   as if with individuals
having a quiddity about them none can reduce to order
Now the whole matter of the city being involved with government as it is
since the isolated communities would at some stage require markets
and markets would lead from economics to politics and to officialdom
whose dwellings   financed out of surpluses   would be banded together
promoting the growth of arts and crafts and other amenities

raises curious problems of federational politics that remain unsolved
and may be of interest to common or garden beings even today
When you think that the Mesoamerican Indians set up religious cities
empire after empire   wash after conquest wash
while each time it appears that the farmers grew weary
of raising sophisticated temples to the leadership's gods
who had a lot to do with mathematics and astronomy
but precious little with their own heads full of weather and maize
so that   as empires crumbled   the farmers let cities choke
going back to the original villages you find them in now
while in other cultures the cities remained open and prospered

you may wonder in what way this puzzle applies to us
who have in our time seen Guernica bombed   London   Dresden   Hanoi
while Paris and Rome have been saved by chance   others by disinvolvement
who witness one way or other the silting up of cities
either with a leprosy of indifferent building or a plague of cars
while in Tokyo or Calcutta it is man himself who clots the streets
What is the praise and aria for the great cities in our time to be
who already suspect their time is passing
man's happiness is gravely endangered by them
his wisdom   needing nothing but patience   no city can grant
while there are hills and valleys to engage his feet

even the leisured have become slaves to entertainments
an interminable conveyor-belt of concerts   plays   shows
the victims of a spray of words every moment of day and night
so that the duty of man to break silence has become a nightmare
the selectors set over us are no wiser than we
the acceleration of culture must drive anyone mad in a bookstore
or faced with the weekly accumulation of solicitations on his desk
in the end it is not the play that is played for us but we who are fed to the play
I know from academics the petrification of language
the murder of enthusiasm   the assassination by compromise
of any idea that strays into the hands of "democratically elected committees"

I know that knowledge has become an industry like the rest
I know how the shoddy costing exactly the same as the good
is invariably chosen in general ignorance and erected with great haste
I know that the massacre of the human environment applies to cities too
and that the most elegant buildings are always the victims
so that I am obliged to wonder when we shall start having Xmas in summer
and the inevitable end of the cities will be upon us
There is gemütlichkeit here and there which compensates for much
especially in Europe but I think it is fast disappearing
because international culture is a uniform now in which prominenz assembles
smoking the latest brand of cigarette

there was an elegance about Vienna   its waltzes
which unsettles the heart   Apollinaire's Paris
still musics in June though the trams have gone
London scones did much for Pound and for Eliot
Joyce and Yeats drank Dublin   MacDiarmid Edinburgh
but when the great have gone who made cities appear
to spread their skirts like temples with resident priesthoods
when it seems the erudition which justifies all this is dying
knowledge of period and place   style   grace in history
my generation is the last to have   going now with computers
stores of disaster and triumph both   which need not choose

then it seems that the fires which have been lit in the cities
the children rummaging through ruins in search of parents
shadows seared into brick like fossil inscriptions
by our mean wars may be trying to warn us
that it is time to trek   to let our feet find earth
to rhyme with nature our congested lives
and this not by smothering the green belts round us with overspills
but by rethinking entirely the relations between society and architecture
Le Corbusier having already said in the nineteen twenties
that architecture properly understood could replace revolution
but they can't even learn here how concrete slobbers under rain

The dogs of Florence are lost   the smells have vanished
the dogs of Dante's city cannot find their way home
water spreads through the streets like brine through the drowned
blood has turned to mud   to printing ink and oil
cars are buffeted around like stones in a kidney
thousands of books unread in all these years
soaked with the Ponte Vecchio rats and worth about as much
the doors of heaven battered   Cimabue annulled
mould spreading over frescoes   poets in a dark wood
and all the sodden history no one had reconstructed
to Monteverdi   to Palestrina perhaps   how much did we want Florence to die

how much would we not have added coal and fall-out to the mixture
seen with an inner glee the mountains collapse over the city
the black tongues lick up children
how much did we not desire the mother's blood to kill the child
the slow stain to spread through its limbs without transfusion
because we no longer have the time to suckle our inheritance
have kept it too long drying below the streets
instead of spreading it over the earth for everyone's comfort
it has gone putrid inside us like a fetus   it drives us mad
if we do not get out again into the fields dear colleagues
how long will it be before we drop the last of the bombs

As Tikal reverts to jungle   the trogon nests on green seas
sublunar Angkor sounds with the ocean's prayers
Selinunte bates into Africa after two thousand years
Venice sinks month by month   her palazzi go blind
Hué's cosmic gardens melt in a tide of rubble
but we cannot begin anew because we have polluted even the sea
birds on their migrations cannot settle   seals cannot mate
the ocean populations drift like ghosts under the slicks
we no longer deal   dear colleagues   with the cankered rose
foul your private garden if you will but you are fouling the world
if a horse shits in China this cow in Wales is besmeared

the tides from the ends of the earth swill our own excrement about our feet

THIRTEEN

We do not remember why this custom is performed in this manner   my lord
any more than we remember the beginnings of earth or sky   our motherfather
we think   he said spitting on his hands and rubbing them together
that father sky came down on mother earth just so   they rubbed together
out of which we Zutuhil may have been born   our motherfather
in the days when you were doubtless one of us but were taken north
where you could not wear these clothes anymore for the cold upon you
You remember the mystery of crucifixion eve enacted here   is it not so
San Juan Bautista and Maria appear to have made love

when they should have been looking for Jesucristo among the Jews
Now you should know whether the holy church was here or not
in Santiago Zutuhil from the beginning of the world
whether or not it was put up with ropes made of womens' hair
while we men lay in the fields as our hoes worked by themselves
How can I tell you   hermanos mios   your tales are confused
the warp and woof of time grievously crossed among you
how can I tell you that you have mashed together the books
of the lords of Quauhtemallan and the laws of my people

when for you the very notion of Jew is something so antediluvian
that nothing like such snakes could roam the world today
when anything claimed to be Indian and Catholic is Catholic
anything said by Catholic priests to the contrary notwithstanding
and this though I have taught a handful of youths some rudiments
of Maya history from the preclassic horizon to Chichén and Uxmal
right up to this very day in these your highlands
little as you wanted to know precisely   to be shown on the maps
when it is so pleasant to ask the same questions over and over

Here we dance the conquista   numb-faced   day after day
hidden behind our masks   golden beards   mustaches
here we stamp drunkenly with the monkeys and bulls

as if the books had never been written   the records set straight

we do not remember why this is so   my lord   our motherfather
we think that it is because our ancestors did it this way
we are afraid that the forgetting of our forgetting should recur

as if the books had never been written   the records set straight

so that to do this or that is to maintain the world
even though our memories no longer know why
we manure the fields at last   we abandon the earth

as if the books had never been written   the records set straight

We are the flowers of the field
    we last one day
        if you wish to take my picture   good
            I die   my picture stays
                here is my child   she is young
                    she is a flower
                        if you wish to take her picture   good
                            her picture remains
                                will you say she dies
                                    will you say she does not die
                                        you cannot tell
                                            look at the burdens
                                                they litter the earth
                                                    we leave the earth behind

I can only assure you   hermanos mios   that the intention counts
I can only admit to you that I myself do not know what I am doing
when a little less drunk than the rest   on this midnight
at about the time that Jesucristo agonized under the olives
I seize the Latin prayerbook you think explains the world
kneel on the straw in the twelve by twelve chapel

slobbering boys weaving the copal smoke around me
and with wide gestures of the cross   a roaring of pig Latin
bless you into your coming year   with a god's hands   hermanos mios

                               In the wombs of women
                        in womens' guts
                    this child rocks
                back to health
            my daughter lasts
      another day

In a meadow of fire with earth in flames under my knees
in an ocean of ice with the extent of ocean frozen solid
at the world's core   out to its fingertips   to its branches
I work myself into a passion of language that would speak to all
in my organic voice   an accident of all's
the discovery of a sound and not its making
and look the masters of the mountains rush to do your biddings
name after name signals their presences   the angels of Spain
the angels of France   the United States   Jerusalem the golden

                In a box
                    as long as memory
                       as short as time
                          my daughter goes
                             we walk behind her
                                 spewing our prayers

When will the time come   masters   you and I
to gather in all the strings to the heart and tie the knot
to breathe   breathe as the birds do   lift up these wings in flight
press water through these gills   leap alongside the salmon
inhale the dank of jungles   crash through the trees with apes
and find at last the silence   man stretching out his palms
to a love once only   a speech once only   a calm   and I saying
that we make eden of these shoots   of these short grasses
that we raise hay in paradise   of praying flowers   praying fruit

My daughter can't return
    she was too young to have a soul
        there is nothing for her to pick up again
            she has no tools
                she will go like the drowned
                    estos jodidos ahogados
                        face down in mud
                            no weaving more   no cooking
                                no sweating in the sweatbath
                                  no opening legs   no love
                                no pains of birth
                                      no crying for her dead
                                      she can't return
                                          my daughter drowned
                                          can she even die

The eagle which faces both ways   my lord   much older than Spain
the snake on which you piss in the grass by mischance
the leaves on which the young gods go mewling to the sea

as if the books had never been written   the records set straight

the dog that looks like a sheep we have never seen hereabouts
two kinds of sardine for which our lake is barely famous
the quickness of our birds   the elegance of creation

as if the books had never been written   the records set straight

our crimson garments   our purples   halos of womens' heads
wizards who somersault three times on leaves and turn to jaguars
a ravishing blonde who wants you quickly like a sow

dying as if the books had not been written   the records set straight

The bulls are dancing on the plaza in front of the church
the horned bulls swilling trago under their vizors
in danger of doing each other damage with their horns
the elders stagger about with their bottles   arm in arm
pointing to the sky with one finger   one God only above
we are going to scream through the streets very soon the elders and I
airing our balls as we go under the influence
repeating over and over again that we do not know the whys and wherefores
I can only assure you   hermanos mios   that the intention counts

weaving through village streets   tripping over the lava
past the round stones of the witches where blood lettings are thrown
truth is intense and intent tonight but not violent
we pass the place where the winds are contained
we celebrate with a little of pipe   a little of drum
truth is intense and intent tonight but not violent
we carefully skirt our navel where the sky rope rises
kiss the vulvas and wombs of the first mothers in a box
truth is intense and intent tonight but not violent

here is the newborn wrapped in the first mothers' rags
rocked in the corn house   the wind house   the smoke house
told about deer and jaguar   though there is no more hunting
told about mother maize his limbs are made of
the bulls dance all night below the church
the Spaniards take out their swords and sharpen them
the bulls' heads are lowered   the trago bottles crash to the ground
in a single act the swords go through the bulls' lungs
the racial memory skewered   all customs fall away

All over the world the horned kings bellow through the night
their great manes swinging   their cojones sweating between their legs
the blind lords in their labyrinths shiver   they take cold

dear God where is her soul   has she a soul to go   where is my daughter

as if the books had never been written   the records set straight

FOURTEEN

I invite you now to lay down your hands
along your sides and lie motionless while the child in your womb
is worked into his obvious   his vulgar birth
without your patting his limbs   smoothing his flesh along the way
or otherwise interfering overmuch in principle's name
for whatever is made as it should be   thus long and hard enough
outlasts contention   the winds of trade   and is

and no one will ever be able to pull in their chest
to suck you   what you have made   into their poverty
It takes a long time to bring to poetry
whatever sears the spirits of any particular age
when each letter   each word   each comma must pass
each breath be submitted to interminable tests
so what we have now is   the age of song is dead

song is laid cold like dick robin in his grave
when there's too much noise for each robin's song to be heard
apart from which I doubt that people care enough
for the details of anyone but a most unaverage self   and they are rare
but few wish to know this or take account of it
very naturally too   one supposes   with the spread of education
Now everyone exhibits all their tools   from chords to private parts

indeed the very complexion of their seed in public
striving to make us all admire the shade and spurt of it
the curdle   the oyster green at the edges   as if by that time
it could still be shot back into their own womb to any purpose
bisexual worms flogging your pottage messes
the most typically loquacious dreaming of tools up backs
paid handsomely to shock the now unshockable

they talk of making every kind of love against the bomb
when what they are going to get if they are not too careful
is several inches of extremely cold steel which will do more than tickle

and by no stretch of the imagination give any kind of pleasure
I say this not because I'm slave to capital
but precisely because revolution still has meaning for me
and the majorities around can't wait for parity

Thus some American delusions though America is where
the English language is growing most energetically in our time
as for the mini-masturbations we drip into our beers
I can hardly believe that they count at all
we are not the genuine inheritance of Brecht and Vallejo
Lorca   Breton   Mandelstam   Rilke   Pessoa
and I doubt you think so either

we stand anywhere on this island a few miles from the sea
but light years away from any general issue
citing particulars   mugging a house-style
if not so inbred that no one can use us
we are so obvious it makes a sparrow yawn
meanwhile we all bemoan the shrinking circle of poetry's influence
but never give a moment's thought at how to get it back

our literary weeklies are still busy keeping Dylan at bay
dead-scared that bloat apocalypse might come riding down the sky
put marsh-tits out of business   sink their tidy decades
move our bowels again until we're sick of movement
so let's get off these cabbage bushes now
us gardeners of the border seedlings   us neo-provincials
and take up again where the first half of the century left off

let's get around to moving our mother in all her positions
open her bed   in this hotel   to all the courants d'air
don't let's worry if it stops us making poems for a while
we must get used to being seen to be doing justice to her
to learn the vulgar tricks we need to keep her happy
we may even grow to love the way she tastes and smells
and fuck private language unless you know   and if you know you're public

FIFTEEN

The elders at the zenith of their power look down the sky
from the decline of the mountain   the ocean slide
the homeward slope   an uninhabited moon
in the path of the westering sun   their hair shining
theirs is forgetfulness   intermittent recognition
remembrances of youth greatly outnumbering recent events
they look down with patience mostly

they range the empty desert   they are few and far between
they go back into the dream companionless
they sit for hours on end throwing their shadows on time
their blood spurts into the earth they worship
they urinate into dishes to mix their paints
their saliva and snot goes into gum for a few tools
with which they keep the earth in movement

If I had not waited for all the bricks to be baked in the kilns
for the measurements of the house to be laid out on plans
if I had not thought of improvements time after time
not given way to desire for larger establishments
with more impressive gardens   a greater variety of flowers
if I had not insisted day in day out on the need for construction above all
if I had recognized the imperfection of created things

and made no more than a living room with table   chair   pen
paper in the table drawers   variable weather on the panes
I would have salvaged much of the life I have slept away
for no matter how long the years at our disposal
how often do we feel for any lasting moment
that we are inhabited by the exact voice of what we need to say
not riding alongside   but upon our voice

You have probably known also the desire to be free of these bones
this envelope of skin   this skin sail full of wind
you have probably wanted to fill your beds with as many lovers as could be heard
above the din of individual love
you have been the curators of your own properties
filled your house with goods that will not talk back
tried to collect the uncollectible world

and yet I am not so sure that this desire to encompass all is vanity
it may be the only effort most of us are allowed to make at wisdom
for if rightly understood the balance of this universe is perfect
there is not a hairbreadth of distinction between our good and our evil
though there be room enough to die when feet tread dreams
I accept the imperfection of man   the impurity of action now
allow it all to come at me in its almost unbearable complexity

let it be my task   my pride   to ride it out like breakers
let me be at its mercy like a swimmer in water   a bird on the wind
that my arms   my wings   might twist and turn in the weathers
let me trust that the sum of our imperfections is the body of justice
whose mould squats in the empty desert awaiting our return
let us lay our single flowers   coffin them down together
let their fruit be ground again   let there be new seed

Among all who cut the knot in the name of sanity   of progress
among the ever more busy hives   the ever proliferating systems
without which this planet cannot take its place in the concourse of planets
who then   charged with the task of preserving language
in this Babel of dialects where none has the desire to legislate any more
but only blindly and efficiently to follow the conventions of his task
shall discriminate   select   unite the corpus of law   if not the poet

being acknowledged at last as maker among makers   master of dialectic
rhyming the fields and cities   scanning the roads
apportioning the harvests   liberating the days
motor of energies   guide of hands   bed of rest
setting her songs to music   her music to the spheres
she has time in the earth her body   she has time to spare
for the most beautiful revolution of all

being acknowledged at last   master of dialectic
when this is going to be a unity of which you have no conception as yet
the earth will have gone over the horizon for good into the stars
the one to one love of men and women be an indulgence of the past
we shall be half fish   a quarter bird   something of animals in love
though keeping the root of man   reclassify the angels among the planets
remember our past lives   set out our futures in their frames

there shall be no separation any more between parents and offspring
the leap-frog generations   the interminable execution of fathers
the suffering of mothers donating sons in war
the anguish of younger brothers unprepared to take their elders' places
the giving away of brides to the holocaust
the offer of children to fire in the streets
the milking of human seed to perpetuate the races

The prophet finds it impossible to live for he who predicts in time
robs himself of his own present and what shall I make of my life
who have brought it to this point in time   to this place
where shall I meet with my existence   where encounter it
among what bones can we come to terms with each other   my death and I
shall I be standing at the door after all those years still ignorant
of how I got there in the first place   still unready to go in

with what voice shall I describe the ceremony of passing out of this incarnation
looking down upon myself in peace a fourscore year man
the great worm may writhe in his hole in the center of the stage
the hero who passed me earlier and transfixed me with his spear
may fight body to body with it   overcome it to birdsong
with the seductive smile   the very smile I had around his age
before going to find his bride on the burning mountain

where do I tell you the secrets a lifetime has stored for you
where can I speak to you face to face if not here
as I prepare to sing out the praises of created things
completely forgetting what cannot be said on their behalf
The rooms of my life grow wide
in all their corners there is room to breathe   there are windows
my house is built upon the labyrinths   the mazes of the worm

I have known the worm too in my time   the worm is not alien to me
I have had the worm in my guts for most of my life
there is no distinction to be made between species of worm
the worm has paraded up and down in me twisting his cocky head
in my childhood science was ignorant   tests always negative
in my maturity society too careless   I writhed daily of the worm
I am a corridor through which the worms pass and take their ease

the worm does not wait for my death to go in and come out of me
he finds his solace in my bed   he makes his breeding ground
he promenades in and out of the bodies of my wife and children
passing from one person to another at a touch of the fingers
almost it seems he passes at the glance of an eye
the worm multiplies in my house as I have less and less years to keep
this is how he lives off me   I do no more than house him

yet I welcome his passage and the beautiful contradictions of his work
the lichen of excrement he leaves in me that excrete him in due time
as a denominator of the flights that we all take through one another
the most material sign of certain processes   some of which are of spirit
All of a sudden life is very beautiful
there is an everbloom in the center of my existence
I want life to go on for ever

Among the blossoms of this floribunda which has forgotten seasons
each of whose individual flowers sucks the paps of justice one by one
as they hang from the bosom of the sky
there is a fruit for each one of you I encounter on my path
and one for each one that I do not encounter
we shall all meet one day on a long lawn   at the age of eighty
and talk over tea or drinks why we did not love each other more

There is a lady in blue with red hair going through a garden in Seurat
she is surrounded with a light of green and blue
she carries a parasol that says everything about the uses of paint
she has collected us together   herded our offerings
she shepherds our lights along in dabs of color
she goes to meet her lover with our souls in her skirts
I think she may be the bride of God going back to her husband

we are her sons here looking up the sky along our white beards
we have waited a long time for her to go back to him
it is strange that we are so much older than she appears to be
as we see her walking with her free hand tucking her gown
toward the husband that has never been painted in any picture
through the rows of multicolored flowers we can no longer number
we can think of no questions for her anymore   nothing we wish her to ask

NOTES

I consider *Beautiful Contradictions*, a poem of the very late Sixties—written from an old world shore, in fact, from the Black Mountains of Wales—to be the first poem of the new life I was about to live in the United States as an American poet. It was inspired by the unexpected discovery of Scotsman Hugh MacDiarmid's all-inclusiveness on the Celtic fringes of English language poetry; by Ezra Pound, a man of Europe as well as America, and by Charles Olson, the prime incarnation for me of the Americanophile wings of American poetry proper, the poetry born of Walt Whitman and Emily Dickinson. Thus a transition from the old world to the new.   [2013]

An outline of the main themes of this poem may be useful to the reader.

The quest for reality starts from primitive innocence (the flower). It continues through every shade of complexity to the exhaustion of human capacities (the fruit). It ends with a new simplicity: the seed of wisdom. Attachment to the particular is given up on behalf of attachment to the general and, finally, of non-attachment. The pursuit of the good life is not incompatible with detachment. But we must remember the earth on which the ideal society is to be set: conservation of nature can be pursued together with social radicalism.

The linear view of history is acceptable within a cyclical one: our own segment of the circle is long enough to appear linear. In the cyclical view, the mother is the abiding reality: incest with her locks us in the past until we have exhausted it. In the linear view, the mother becomes the daughter—in whose sight, if we can restore it, history will proceed. Fathers and sons, primitives as well as sages: we re-enter Eden, out of which we seem to have been driven, with the whole world on our backs.

Anthropologists are often torn between their desire to preserve what they study and their knowledge that the clock can never be turned back. For them, scientific records serve as a formal constraint, as well as a point of departure, for the imagination and faithful topography may be very near to the concept of justice.

In the following detailed notes, I attempt to deal only with areas of knowledge that may be unfamiliar to the general reader.   [1969]

Section Two

Line 8:   The Zutuhil Maya Indians of Santiago Atitlán, Guatemala, believe in a line of reincarnating rain priests who help them in times of trouble. *Ralkoal Zutuhil:* son of the Zutuhil.

Line 10: *cofradía:* a chapel for Catholic saints (*santos*). *Alcalde, juez,* etc.: titles of *cofradía* officials.

Line 15: *traguito:* a potent alcohol. Drinking, smoking and dancing are regarded as "services" performed in the saint's honor.

Line 16: Some saints are compounded with pre-Columbian deities. The *Maximón* or *Mam* is a piece of wood, normally kept in a bundle, which is clothed on fiestas to form a large puppet. *Mam,* the "Old God," who died and was reborn with the year, became associated with Easter, when he represents Judas Iscariot.

Line 17: Pedro de Alvarado took *Tziquinahá* ("House, or water, of birds"), capital of the ancient Zutuhil, in 1524. *Quauhtemallan:* the old form of "Guatemala."

Line 26: In other parts of the area, Judas is burned after the Easter rites.

Line 27: In *cofradía San Martín,* associated with wild beasts, the doors must be kept closed during rituals to prevent the world's winds from escaping.

Line 31: Official Catholic antagonism to the *Mam* is a feature of recent Atiteco history.

Line 33: The *Mam* is associated with witchcraft and love-magic.

Line 39: *Huracán* and other old deities occur in the *Popol Vuh* of the neighboring Quiché Maya: see A. Recinos (editor), University of Oklahoma Press, Norman, 1950, and Dennis Tedlock (editor and translator), Simon and Schuster, New York, 1985.

Line 50: *Maltiosh te-e-taa,* etc.: Ritual salutations to fellow officials before a drink can be taken.

Section Three

Line 1:   Current anthropological theory of matrilineal societies has influenced this section.

Line 25: Africa-Europe is one unit here, flowing toward America as slavery. Charles Olson's *Call Me Ishmael* is an important source.

Line 51: Underground locust frescoes: Cholula pyramids, Central Mexico.

Section Four

Line 10: The reference is to Siegfried and Brünnhilde in Wagner's *Ring of the Nibelung.* Siegfried here is also Oedipus and Tiresias.

Section Five

Line 21: St. James of Compostela (Santiago) is the patron of Santiago Atitlán.

Section Six
Line 4: The hero is a compound of Oedipus, Orpheus and the Christ.
Line 22: Alternate lines are from statements by war-crime defendants in World War II trials.

Section Seven
Line 11: *Singing-Birds:* a farm in the Black Mountains of Brecknockshire where this poem was composed.

Section Eight
Line 3: The Ajantā caves, north of Bombay, are sometimes visited by Tibetan monks.
Line 13: The Mahāyāna Buddhist "Perfection of Wisdom" (*Prajñāpāramitā*) holds that the enlightened are able to understand both the saving of individuals by Bodhisattvas—who postpone Buddhahood until they have saved others—as well as the fact that there are no Bodhisattvas, or persons to be saved, except in the realm of appearances.
Line 25: *Sangha:* The Order of Buddhist monks. *Sangha* can mean the whole Order (*Sangha* of Four Quarters) or a local sub-group.
Line 30: Gifts to monks mean sowing good deeds in order to reap merit.
Line 32: Ideally, a monk's robe should be of shreds and patches.
Line 49: *Aberfan:* Welsh site of a major mining disaster in the late sixties.

Section Nine
Line 26: *Amitābha:* The Buddha of the western paradise in the Sino-Japanese "Buddhism of Faith."

Section Ten
Line 1: In medieval iconography, the Triumphant Church is often paired with the Defeated Synagogue, shown blindfolded and carrying a broken staff.
Line 24: For Kabbalistic and Hassidic Judaism, see G. Scholem: *Major Trends in Jewish Mysticism*.
Line 40: See Pierre Jean Jouve's poem *"Songe."*
Line 49: The Garden of Eden picture in the *"Très Riches Heures du Duc de Berry."*
Line 60: The *Staronová:* a thirteenth century synagogue in the Prague ghetto. Kafka lived nearby. Rabbi Loew, legendary creator of the Golem (a precursor of Frankenstein) is buried in the Old Jewish Cemetery up the street.
Line 102: *aleph:* first letter of the Hebrew alphabet.

Section Eleven

Line 1: For the medieval map kept in Hereford Cathedral, see Konrad Miller: *Mappae Mundi*, vol. IV, Stuttgart, 1895-8. Widespread animal and monster-lore derives from Pliny and Solinus, while wind-lore is found in Isidore of Seville's *Etymologiarum sive originum*.

Line 5: Norman French: "Look, my Son, on the flesh of which thou art made / and the breasts from which you drank a Virgin's milk."

Line 9: *Gades Herculis*: the Straits of Gibraltar. C.f. line 25 in Section Three.

Line 12: *Sandaliotes*: Sardinia, shaped like a sandal.

Line 13: Lipari was regarded as a shortcut to Hell.

Line 16: Joseph was thought to have stored his crops in the Pyramids.

Line 45: Gog and Magog are probably the Chinese whom Alexander is said to have kept out of Europe.

Line 67: Caesar and the Father God are compounded here, enthroned at the eastern top of the map. Jerusalem is at the center.

Line 76: Lake Atitlán is (wrongly) reputed to be surrounded by twelve villages named after the Apostles.

Line 79: Régis Debray's list of fallen guerillas was published in Havana, January 1968. Guevara's nickname, "the Prince," came from a habit of wearing black gloves when doing manual labor.

Section Twelve

Line 1: New Granada included the lands of Hopi, Zuni and other Pueblo Indians of Arizona and New Mexico.

Line 13: John Martin (1789–1854) illustrated *Paradise Lost*.

Line 25: Some have thought that the great jungle cities of the Lowland Maya witnessed a revolt of the lower classes and were slowly abandoned.

Line 111: *Tikal*: a Classic Maya site in the Peten jungle, Guatemala. The trogon here is the quetzal, national bird of Guatemala.

Line 113: *Selinunte*: a Greek site in Southern Sicily.

Section Thirteen

Line 25: *Chichén Itzá* and *Uxmal*: two late Maya sites, Yucatán, Mexico.

Line 29: Masked men, representing Spaniards, Indians, demons and animals, re-enact the Spanish Conquest at Indian *fiestas*.

Line 51: Pre-Columbian "Year-Bearer" deities carried Time on their backs for specified periods. Contemporary Atitecos carry social duties as "burdens" in the same way.

Line 60: *copal*: an incense.

Line 63: *Cofradía San Martín* contains a bundle of sacred maize cakes and a box full of rags, representing the "tripes" (wombs) of the first women. Sick children are rocked in the box.

Line 75:   *Mam*, when young, is plural and male / female. These are both *dueños* (lords) of hills, winds, rains, animals etc. and Christian angels. Spain, the U.S. and Jerusalem sum up the external world. France was added for the author's benefit.
Line 98:   *estos jodidos ahogados*: those fucking drowned. The drowned have and give a bad time after death.
Line 108: *Klau-Koj*: a two-headed eagle thought to be pre-Columbian rather than a Hapsburg importation.
Line 112: A poodle.

Section Fourteen
Line 50:   Dylan here is Dylan Thomas. This section refers to poetry in Britain though much of it could apply to Anglophile poetry in the U.S.

Section Fifteen
Line 8:   The primeval "moulds" here are Australian aborigines even though anthropology, after Durkheim, has ceased to regard them as the "most primitive" people on earth.
Line 87:   Siegfried, in *The Ring*, kills a great dragon, or *Wurm*.
Line 127: Study for *La Grande-Jatte*, Kunstmuseum, Göteborg.
Line 130: The *Shekhinah*, or female aspect of God in the Kabbalah, reunites the light principles scattered in souls at the end of Time. Scholem mentions a late view of her, in exile and weeping for Israel, as "the beauty who no longer has eyes."